LITERATURE LIST

• *Very Last First Time*
by Jan Andrews;
Macmillan 1986. (PS-1)
Canadian distribution by Distican.
A story of the Inuit people of Northern
Canada. Eva's first time searching under
the ice for shellfish nearly turns to
disaster when she dallies too long.

• *Ida and the Wool Smugglers*
by Sue Ann Alderson;
Macmillan 1986.(1-3)
Canadian distribution by Distican.
Ida saves sheep from smugglers in this
pioneer story set in western Canada.

• *A Dog Came, Too: A True Story*
by Ainslee Manson;
Macmillan 1993. (1-3)
Canadian distribution by Distican.
A fictionalized story of the dog that
accompanied explorer Alexander
Mackenzie across Canada.

• *Chester's Barn*
by Lindee Climo;
Tundra paper 1982. (2-4)
The story in words and pictures of life in
a Prince Edward Island barn on a winter
afternoon.

• *Mary of Mile 18*
by Ann Blades;
Tundra paper 1971. (2-4)
Mile 18 is in reality a Mennonite
community in Canada, and Mary was a
student in the school where the author
taught.

• *Children of the Yukon*
by Ted Harrison;
Tundra paper 1977. (2-4)
Life in present-day Yukon with a little
historical material.

• *A Candle for Christmas*
by Jean Speare;
Macmillan 1987. (2-4)
Canadian distribution by Distican.
Tomas's parents must leave him but promise
to be back by Christmas Eve in this story of
the Canadian Northwest.

• *Yukon River: An Adventure to the Gold
   Fields of the Klondike*
by Peter Lourie;
Boyd Mills 1992. (3-6)
Canadian distribution by McClelland &
   Stewart.
Following the route of prospectors in the
1890s, this book takes the reader on a trip
down the Yukon by canoe.

• *The City Girl Who Went to Sea*
by Rosemarie Hausherr;
Macmillan 1990. (3-5)
Canadian distribution by Distican.
Alicia, a city girl, visits a remote village in
Newfoundland in 1977.

• *Inuit*
by Bryan & Cherry Alexander;
Raintree LB 1993. (3-6)
Canadian distribution by Saunders Book Co.
An introduction to the Eskimo people of the
world, with emphasis on those in Canada
and Greenland.

GEOGRAPHY

Historical Aid

Canada is the second-largest nation in the world, with a land area of almost 10 million square kilometers (3,860,000 square miles). Much of the land is in or near the arctic regions, making it almost uninhabitable, and there are still large areas of undeveloped wilderness. The vast central prairies are rich in farmland. The remaining land is rich in natural resources—fish, furs, timber, and minerals. The landscape is covered with numerous lakes and waterways.

Canada is made up of 11 provinces—Alberta, British Columbia, Manitoba, New Brunswick, Newfoundland, Nova Scotia, Nunavut, Ontario, Prince Edward Island, Quebec, Saskatchewan; and two territories—the Yukon and Northwest Territories. Each area has its own distinctive characteristics and economy.

Project

Make a map of Canada.

Directions

1. Color the map pattern, coloring each province and territory a different color.

2. Use the atlas to identify the capital cities of each province/territory and add them to the map, marking each with a star.

3. Add geographical details like rivers, lakes, and mountain ranges.

*In 1999, the Northwest Territories will be divided. The eastern portion will be named Nunavut, and the western portion will still be called the Northwest Territories.

Materials

• Map pattern, following page
• Colored pencils
• Atlas or a map of Canada

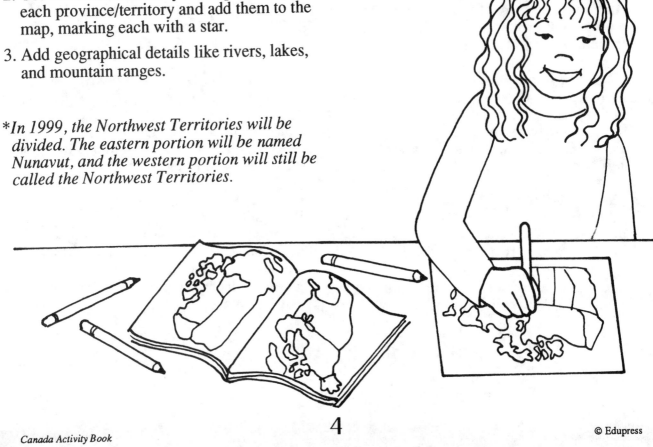

Canada

ACTIVITY BOOK

Exploring a Culture Through Art, Crafts, Cooking, Games, and Historical Aids

Authors	Linda Milliken
	Kathy Rogers
Editor	Kathy Rogers
Page Design	Kathy Rogers
Cover Design	Brent Harder
Illustrations	Barb Lorseyedi

METRIC CONVERSION CHART

Refer to this chart when metric conversions are not found within the activity.

1 ml	=	¼	tsp	1 ml	=	¼	tsp	
2 ml	=	½	tsp	180° C	=	350° F		
5 ml	=	1	tsp	190° C	=	375° F		
15 ml	=	1	Tbsp	200° C	=	400° F		
60 ml	=	¼	cup	216° C	=	425° F		
80 ml	=	⅓	cup					
125 ml	=	½	cup	2.54 cm	=	1	in	
250 ml	=	1	cup	30 cm	=	1	ft	
				91 cm	=	1	yd	
28 g	=	1	oz	1.6 cm	=	1	mile	
.45 kg	=	1	lb					

EP077 • ©1997, 2002 Edupress, Inc.™ • P.O. Box 883 • Dana Point, CA 92629
www.edupressinc.com
ISBN 1-56472-077-2
Printed in USA

Table of Contents

Canada Activity Book

5

Maple Leaf

Historical Aid

The sugar maple grows across Canada from Newfoundland to Manitoba. It can be found as far south as the Great Lakes. Sugar maples may reach a height of 41 meters (135 ft). The trunk of an individual tree may be 1.5 meters (5 ft) across. The sugar maple has gray bark and dark-green leaves. In autumn the leaves turn to yellow, orange, and red.

The hard wood of the maple tree provided much of the lumber from which Canadian settlers built their homes. During the 1700s and 1800s maple sugar ranked as an important food item. People traded it for various foods and services. The importance of the maple tree to the growth of Canada was recognized in 1860 when the maple leaf was made the official emblem of Canada.

Project

Use the maple leaf patterns to create a variety of maple leaf art projects.

Materials

• Maple leaf patterns (page 8)
• Materials as listed for each project

Autumn Maple Leaves

Materials

• White construction paper
• Red, yellow, orange crayons
• Watercolor paints and brushes
• Scissors

Directions

1. Cut out the maple leaf patterns.

2. Use the crayons to trace several in an overlapping pattern onto white construction paper. Retrace the outline of each leaf by pressing heavily with the crayons.

3. Paint a watercolor wash in shades of yellow, orange, and red over the outlined leaves.

Maple Leaf

Maple Leaf Border

Materials

- White construction paper
- Red butcher paper
- Scissors • Glue
- Crayons • Tape

Directions

1. Trace and cut out a maple leaf from white construction paper.

2. Color a self-portrait in the center of the maple leaf.

3. Cut long strips of butcher paper, 15.25 cm (6 in) wide.

4. Glue all the maple leaves side-by-side on the butcher paper. Tape the border to the classroom wall.

Maple Leaf Mobile

Materials

- Wire hanger • Yarn
- Scissors • Starch
- Hole punch • Paint brush
- Canadian travel brochures and magazines

Directions

1. Use the largest maple leaf pattern to outline three to five leaves on colorful pictures of Canada.

2. Cut out the leaves and punch a hole in the top of each.

3. Paint a layer of starch over each side of the leaf. Allow to dry.

4. Cut yarn into various lengths and tie one end through the leaf and the other around the hanger.

5. Hang the mobile from the ceiling.

Maple Leaf Pattern

8

Canadian Flag

Historical Aid

In 1964, Prime Minister Lester Pearson proposed a new Canadian flag. At that time, Canada used the Red Ensign, which included the British Union Jack, as its national flag. A parliamentary committee recommended a flag with an 11-point maple leaf in a broad white center stripe with a broad vertical red stripe at each end.

Because the proposed flag contained no reminders of Canada's ties with Great Britain, some Canadians felt it was designed to reduce French resentment toward the English. The Canadian Parliament debated the flag issue for 33 days. Parliament adopted the new flag in December and it became Canada's official flag on February 15, 1965.

Project

Make a collection box that features a Canadian flag on the lid.

Materials

- Red and white construction paper
- Maple leaf patterns (Page 8)
- Shoe box
- Scissors
- Glue
- Pencil

Directions

1. Cover a shoe box and its lid with white construction paper.

2. Trace a maple leaf onto red construction paper. Cut out the leaf and glue it to the center of the lid.

3. Cut two wide strips of red construction paper and glue them to the shoe box lid on both sides of the maple leaf.

4. Begin a collection of postcards, newspaper articles, and other memorabilia that focus on Canada. Take time to share the contents of the storage box "flags" as the school year progresses.

Coat of Arms

Historical Aid

There are ten Canadian provinces and two territories. Each of the provinces and territories has an identifying flag and floral emblem. All have a coat of arms which tells a story about that province or territory.

For example, the provincial coat of arms for Alberta, adopted in 1907, features the cross of St. George, symbolizing Alberta's historic association with Great Britain. Mountains and foothills stand for the Canadian Rockies. A field of wheat at the bottom represents Alberta's chief agricultural crop.

Project

Create a border, photo essay, or poster featuring one or all of the provincial and territorial coats of arms.

Materials

- Coat of Arms coloring pages, following
- Construction paper or poster board
- Crayons or colored pencils
- Scissors
- Glue

Directions

1. Reproduce the coloring pages so that each person completing a project has 13 coats of arms.
2. Using crayons or colored pencils, follow the color guides below each coat of arms.
3. Cut around the outline of each.
4. Arrange the coats of arms on a poster board or strips of construction paper placed end to end to create a decorative border. Identify each one.

Extended Activity

- *Research each provincial or territorial flag and floral emblem. Illustrate them in a mini-picture book that includes historical facts.*

Quebec Prince Edward Island Saskatchewan Northwest Territory

Coat of Arms

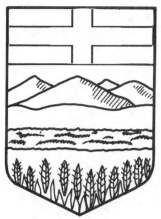

Alberta

red cross; blue sky; white mountains; green hills;
blue and white water; yellow fields

British Columbia

gold lion; brown elk; white sheep; red and gold crown;
blue and red Union Jack; blue and white waves; gold sun

Manitoba

red cross on white; gold buffalo; gold
ground; green background

Nunavut

red and gold crown; white igloo, caribou,
narwhal; yellow spheres, stars on blue; blue
inuksuk, black lamp on yellow

New Brunswick

red and gold crown; yellow lion on red;
white sail; red ship flags; brown ship on
yellow background; blue water

Nova Scotia

white shield with gold and red emblem, dark blue cross bars;
white unicorn, brown mane; light blue feathers

Ontario

red cross; brown animals; gold maple leaves;
green shield; gold banner

Canada Activity Book

11

© Edupress

COAT of ARMS

Prince Edward Island
gold lion on orange; yellow banner;
green trees and grass on white

Quebec
red, gold and green crown; yellow fleur-de-lis on blue;
yellow lion on red; green maple leaves on yellow; white banner

Saskatchewan
red lion on yellow;
yellow wheat on green background

Yukon Territories
red cross on white; blue emblems on white circle; gold dots; red
triangles; white wavy lines on blue; white dog on red and gold bar

Northwest Territories
wavy blue line on white; gold bars on green field;
white fox on red; gold Arctic whales

Newfoundland
red shield with white cross; animals in upper right and lower left
sections white, the other two brown; brown elk at top

Regional Food

Historical Aid

The many cultures that have contributed to the growth of Canada have also added to the variety of foods enjoyed by the people that live there. The early inhabitants of Canada ate off the land, adapting native plants and animals to their use. Inuits enjoyed eating *muktuk* (whale skin and blubber).

Today, each region of the country has its specialties—British Columbia and the Maritime Provinces are known for seafood; the Prairies are known for their excellent beef; Quebec has developed a distinctive French-Canadian style; in the Northwest Territories moose meat and fresh lake fish are popular.

Project

Plan a feast and sample foods that are popular in Canada.

Materials

- White paper tablecloth
- Red tempera paint and paint brush
- Maple leaf pattern (page 8)
- Poster board   • Scissors
- See individual recipes for ingredients

Directions

1. Use maple leaf pattern and scissors to make a stencil from poster board.
2. With tempera paint and brush, stencil a maple leaf pattern to decorate table cloth.
3. Use the maple leaf theme to make other room decorations.
4. Break into groups for preparation of the recipes. See individual recipes for directions.

Habitant Pea Soup
This is a French-Canadian dish, and was adapted from the traditional food carried by **voyageurs** *on their long trips.*

Ingredients
550 g (1¼ lbs) dried green peas
225 g (½ lb) salt pork
2.5 l (11 cups) water
120 ml (½ cup) chopped celery
60 ml (¼ cup) chopped parsley

2 diced onions
3 bay leaves
5 ml (1 tsp) pepper
5 ml (1 tsp) savory

Directions

1. Wash and drain peas and put them in a soup pot with water. Boil for two minutes; remove from heat and cool for two hours.

2. Add remaining ingredients. Bring soup to a boil again, then turn down heat and simmer two hours.

REgioNAl Food

Tourtiere
Tourtiere is a pork pie that is a traditional favorite in the province of Quebec.

Ingredients

907 g (2 lbs) ground pork
1 clove garlic, crushed
1 medium onion, chopped
120 ml (½ cup) water

1.23 ml (¼ tsp) celery salt
1.23 ml (¼ tsp) ground cloves
Pastry for double-crust pie shell
60 ml (¼ cup) dry bread crumbs

Directions

1. Combine all ingredients except bread crumbs and pastry shell in saucepan.

2. Add salt and pepper to taste.

3. Simmer until meat and onions are tender, about 20 minutes. Stir in bread crumbs and let cool.

4. Line pie pan with half of pastry and cover with pork filling. Cover with other half of pastry and cut vent holes.

5. Bake at 175° C (350° F) until browned, about 35 minutes. Let sit several minutes before serving.

Bannock
This bread was first made by the Native People, who baked it over an open fire. European settlers fried it in a pan.

Ingredients

500 ml (2 cups) flour
500 ml (2 cups) water
Pinch salt
15 ml (1 Tbsp) baking powder

1 egg
15 ml (1 Tbsp) sugar
Vegetable oil

Directions

1. Mix flour, water, salt, and baking powder in a large bowl. Add egg and sugar, mixing well.

2. Heat a small amount of oil in frying pan. Pour one-third of batter into pan and cook until small bubbles appear. Add more oil and flip bannock over. Cook until second side is done.

3. Repeat with remaining batter.

4. Cut bannocks into pieces and serve with jam.

Maple Syrup Shortbreads
It takes 151 l (40 gallons) of maple sap to make 4.5 l (1 gallon) of pure maple syrup.

Ingredients

118 ml (½ cup) butter
60 ml (¼ cup) sugar
236 ml (1 cup) flour
177 ml (¾ cup) brown sugar
118 ml (½ cup) maple syrup

15 ml (1 Tbsp) butter, at room temperature
1 egg, at room temperature
5 ml (1 tsp) vanilla
118 ml (½ cup) chopped nuts

Directions

1. Cream 118 ml (½ cup) butter and sugar in large mixing bowl, using spoon or electric mixer. Add flour, a little at a time, mixing continually, and blend well. Do not form into ball.

2. Pat mixture into bottom of greased 20 cm (8 in) baking pan. Bake at 175° C (350° F) about 25 minutes, or until light brown.

3. In medium bowl blend brown sugar, maple syrup, and butter. Add egg and vanilla and mix until smooth. Pour evenly over shortbread and sprinkle with nuts. Return to oven and bake until topping sets, about 20 minutes. Cool completely and cut into 3.8 cm (1½ in) squares.

Canadian Apple Cake
Apples and maple syrup are two of Canada's most plentiful products.

Ingredients

354 ml (1½ cups) sifted flour
118 ml (½ cup) sugar
5 ml (1 tsp) baking powder
2.5 ml (½ tsp) salt
118 ml (½ cup) shortening
118 ml (½ cup) milk

1 egg, beaten
3 apples, peeled, cored and finely sliced
2.5 ml (2 tsp) ground cinnamon
30 ml (2 Tbsp) butter
30 ml (2 Tbsp) maple syrup

Directions

1. Sift flour, 45 ml (3 Tbsp) sugar, baking powder, and salt in mixing bowl. Cut in shortening with two knives or pastry blender. Stir in milk and eggs to form a soft dough.

2. Spread dough smoothly in 20 cm (8 in) square baking pan and put overlapping slices of apple in rows on the dough. Mix remaining sugar and cinnamon and sprinkle over apples. Dot with butter. Bake at 190° C (375° F) for about 50 minutes or until toothpick comes out clean when inserted in cake. Remove from oven and pour maple syrup over top.

Animals

Historical Aid

Mountains and wastelands make up more than half the land area of Canada, and forests cover about one-third. Although this vast land is home to thousands of kinds of wildlife, some have become endangered due to over-hunting and the destruction of their ecosystem.

The Canadian government has set aside large land areas to create national parks where wildlife and their habitats are protected. Laws restricting hunting and trapping have saved some species, such as sea otters, from extinction.

Project

Choose an animal project to complete.

Animal Diorama

Project

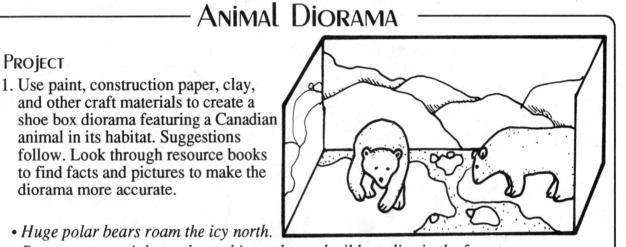

1. Use paint, construction paper, clay, and other craft materials to create a shoe box diorama featuring a Canadian animal in its habitat. Suggestions follow. Look through resource books to find facts and pictures to make the diorama more accurate.

- *Huge polar bears roam the icy north.*
- *Beaver, otter, mink, muskrat, chipmunks, and wildcats live in the forests.*
- *Caribou, moose, and elk roam freely in the wilderness. Deer are a common sight as well.*
- *Moose, bighorn sheep, black and grizzly bears, and mountain goats are among the animals that live in the Rockies.*
- *High forests are home to porcupines, chipmunks, and mountain lions.*
- *Rain forests abound with species such as the cougar, bald eagle, and marmot.*
- *Many types of birds, including sparrows, robins, sea gulls, owls, and quail, make their nests in marshy swamps or forests.*
- *Lakes are filled with herring, perch, and whitefish. The oceans are filled with cod, scallops, salmon, and lobsters.*

Animals

Canada Goose

The Canada goose grows 89 to 109 cm (35 to 43 in) long and has a greyish-brown coat and white patches on its cheeks. Its head, neck and tail are black. It uses twigs, weeds, grass, and reeds to make its nest on a mound in a marsh. It lines its nest with downy feathers. The nest holds from five to nine pale green, yellowish, or buff-white eggs. In the autumn, their distinctive honking can be heard as the families migrate south for the winter months in a perfect V-formation.

Project

1. Use tempera paint to sponge paint a landscape background of a marsh or sky.

2. When the background paint has dried, cut and glue construction paper to create the nest of a Canada goose, or depict a family of geese flying south in a V-formation. Add dimension by gluing twigs and weeds over the eggs, or cotton in the sky.

Beaver

*The beaver, a Canadian national symbol, is found in rivers, streams, and fresh-water lakes near woodlands. An excellent swimmer, a beaver can swim underwater for .8 km (.5 miles) and can hold its breath for 15 minutes. A beaver uses its tail to steer when it swims; as a prop when it stands on its hind legs; and, by slapping it on the water to make a loud noise, as a warning signal. Its teeth are sharp and hard and can cut down small trees. Beaver fur is soft and shiny. Its color varies from shiny dark brown to yellowish brown. When beaver fur is squeezed together with other kinds of fur to make a cloth it is called **felt**.*

Project

1. Paint a background scene on white construction paper that shows something a beaver might be doing: swimming underwater; building a dam or lodge; cutting down a tree; slapping its tail on the water.

2. Paint a beaver in the scene. Cut a felt tail for the beaver and glue it in place in the painting.

The Mounties

Historical Aid

The Mounties, or the Royal Canadian Mounted Police, have become as much a symbol of Canada as the beaver and the maple leaf. The Mounties were originally recruited in 1873 to prevent bloodshed between whisky traders and Native People in the Northwest Territories. Riding horseback, they brought law and order to the expanding Canadian frontier.

The distinctive red coats of the Mounties were a symbol of peace; the color was chosen because the Native People equated red with justice and fair dealing. The broad-brimmed hats were adopted by 1900 because they offered protection from the sun. The Mounties of today still wear the red coat for dress and ceremonial occasions, including magnificent parades.

Project

Make a Royal Canadian Mounted Police puppet.

Materials

- Poster board
- Puppet pattern, following
- Crayons or markers
- Scissors
- Glue
- Paint stirrer or other flat stick

Directions

1. Reproduce puppet pattern. Color and cut out.

2. Glue cut-out onto poster board and trim to shape.

3. Use glue to mount puppet to paint stirrer.

4. Use puppets to stage a play or ceremonial parade.

The Mounties

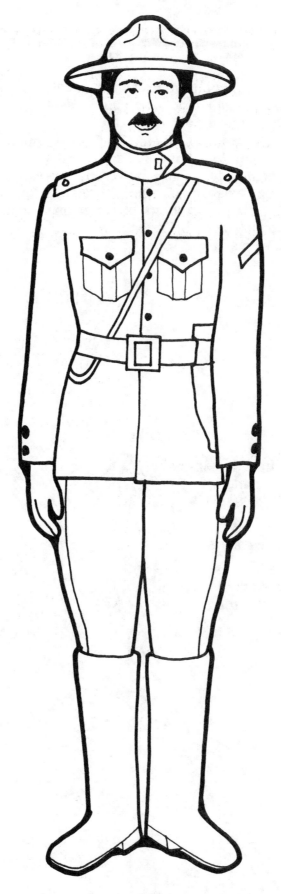

Sports

Historical Aid

The people of Canada are enthusiastic about sports for all seasons. Hockey and other ice sports, as well as baseball and lacrosse, are an important part of Canadian life.

Some sports, like curling, were imported from other nations, but others were developed in Canada. Lacrosse, Canada's national game, evolved from *baggataway*, a game played by the Algonquins of the St. Lawrence River Valley as a way of training warriors for battle. Ice hockey was invented in the 1850s by soldiers in Kingston, Ontario. The rules for another world-popular sport, basketball, were drawn up in 1891 by James Naismith, a Canadian.

Project

Plan a Sports Day to learn and demonstrate Canadian sports.

Materials

- Rule books and sports equipment for suggested games, following

Directions

1. Select which games will be demonstrated and gather necessary equipment.

2. Divide into groups. Each group will be responsible for mastering the skills and safety regulations for one game.

3. Create a schedule that allows students to rotate through the game areas, learning and playing as they rotate through.

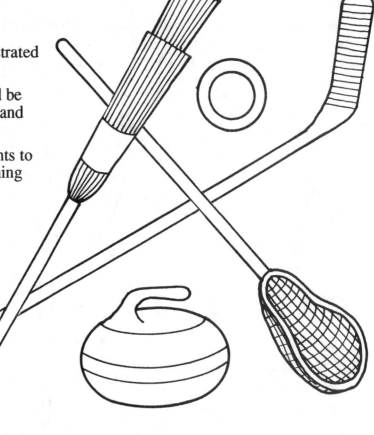

Hockey

The soldiers who first developed this game used a lacrosse ball and field-hockey sticks. Later, players used a wooden disk or cow's kneecap as a puck. Originally it was played with as many players as wanted to participate, and the game was over when a team made three goals or if a player fell through the ice.

A hockey team is made up of six players. Players score points by hitting a round disk called a puck into the goal cage or net. Hockey is exciting and fast-paced. It has become very popular in many countries, especially Russia, Czechoslovakia, Sweden, and the United States.

Lacrosse

Lacrosse was developed in Canada and has become popular throughout Australia, England, and the United States. The game originated with the Native People of Canada, and often involved thousands of players.

The object of lacrosse is to score a goal by throwing, scooping, or kicking a rubber ball into the opposing team's goal. The ball is moved with a stick that has a net pocket at one end. It is the stick that gives lacrosse its name—*la crosse*, French for *the crook*. The ball used is slightly smaller than a baseball, and can travel up to 160.9 km (100 miles) per hour.

Ringette

Ringette is very similar to ice hockey and is usually played by girls and women. It was invented in Ontario, Canada, and is now played in the northern United States as well as some European countries.

Teams of six skaters try to score goals by pushing a hollow rubber ring into a goal net on either end of the ice rink. Ringette sticks are straight on the end, not curved like hockey sticks. No body contact is allowed. As in hockey, protective equipment such as knee and elbow pads and helmets with face masks are worn.

Curling

Another ice sport, curling, was brought to Canada from Scotland in 1759. Curling was developed in Scotland and the Netherlands around 400 years ago. Four-skater teams slide granite stones down an ice rink, aiming toward a 3.7 m (12 ft) target or *house*.

The 19.3 kg (14½ lb) stone is flung first by its handle. The ice in front of the stone is "swept" by team members to decrease any resistance for the stone during its movement into the house. When the stone is flung, it "curls," giving the game its name. Points are scored for the stones landing closest to the center of the house.

Canada Day

Historical Aid

    Canadians celebrate their country's birthday on July 1. Canada Day used to be called Dominion Day. The celebration began on July 1, 1867, when the provinces of Ontario, Quebec, Nova Scotia, and New Brunswick united to form one country. The other provinces and territories joined later. Giant birthday parties throughout the country are given in celebration. Some communities share a large birthday cake. Others put on a fireworks display. Choirs sing, bands play, and dancers perform.

Project

Plan and carry out a birthday celebration that includes traditional activities.

Materials

- Gather the materials listed for each activity and project.

Plan a Parade

- Design simple floats. Decorate wagons or bicycles with patriotic colors and symbols.
- Create a banner to head the parade.
- Choose some patriotic music to play during the parade.
- Dress in costumes that reflect the history of Canada. Your parade should include explorers, trappers, soldiers, and "Mounties."
- Plan a parade route and invite other classes to come and watch.

Canada Day

"Bake" a Cake

- Design a huge paper cake to display on the classroom wall. Cut the cake from butcher paper. Use paint or construction paper to decorate it with national colors. Figure out how many candles should be on the cake.

Choreograph a Dance

- Listen to patriotic music and marches. Select one song and create a dance to perform.

Be Creative

- Create a birthday card for Canada.
- Write a cooperative Big Book. Let each page illustrate an event in Canada's history.
- "Shop" for a special birthday gift. What would you like to give Canada for its birthday? Look through catalogs and magazines. Cut out the picture and glue it to construction paper. Explain to classmates why you chose this particular gift.

VICTORIA DAY

Historical Aid

May 24th marks the birthday of Queen Victoria, the British sovereign who was queen when Canada was established by Great Britain in 1867. Since that event, her birthday has been celebrated in various ways. At one rural post, Mounties staged a snake-killing competition! Victorians of the late nineteenth century held a regatta of small craft. Victoria Day officially became a holiday in 1952, and is celebrated either on May 24th or on the Monday preceding it. Today it is traditionally celebrated with great displays of fireworks. On the same day, people in Quebec celebrate *Fete de Dollard des Ormeaux* honoring a soldier killed during colonial times.

Queen Victoria never visited Canada, yet her influence is still in evidence. It was Queen Victoria who chose Ottawa as the capital of Canada, and the province of Alberta was named for her daughter.

Project

Make a crown in honor of the British monarch Queen Victoria.

Extended Activity

- *Hold a contest in which teams try to locate city and provincial names and other Canadian heritage locales and events which are named for Queen Victoria or a member of her family.*

Materials

- Crown pattern (page 25)
- Large sheet white construction paper
- Aluminum foil
- Gold spray paint or yellow tempera paint
- Scissors
- Tape
- Pencil
- Paint brush

Directions

1. Cut out the crown pattern.

2. Trace two times onto construction paper. Cut out and tape the two pieces together to form a circle.

3. Cover the crown with aluminum foil pressed into shape.

4. Spray with gold paint or brush with yellow tempera paint to create a copper effect.

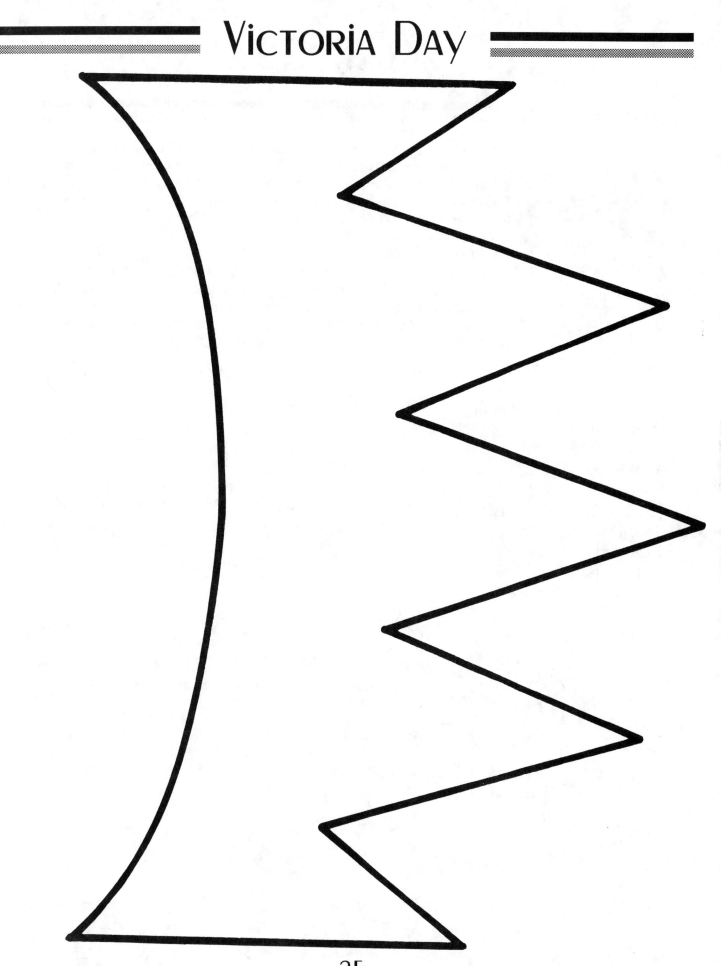

Vikings

Historical Aid

In 1961, archeologists discovered the ruins of a Viking settlement at L'Anse aux Meadows, on the northern tip of Newfoundland. Historians believe that the village may have been settled by Norse adventurer Leif Eriksson. The village was made up of seven turf huts, two large fire pits for roasting caribou and whale, and a smithy with a stone anvil for working iron and copper. It is believed that the village housed between 100 and 140 people.

The Norse were very skilled sailors. Without the use of a compass they could sail from Norway to North America and never be more than 322 km (200 miles) from land. During daylight hours they navigated with a bearing dial. At night they navigated by observing the position of the North Star.

Project

Make a bearing dial and learn to read it.

Materials

- Toilet paper tube
- 15.25 cm (6 in) paper plate
- Toothpicks
- 1 egg carton section
- Marking pen
- Scissors • Glue

Directions

1. Use the marking pen to divide the paper plate into four equal sections. Mark directions as shown.

2. Use toilet paper tube to trace a hole in the center of plate and cut out, being sure that the tube fits snugly in the hole. Slide plate down tube about one-quarter of the length.

3. Trim egg carton section to fit the top of toilet paper tube. Break toothpick in half, inserting one piece in top of section and one in side of section as illustrated. Glue toothpicks to secure.

4. Glue egg carton section onto top of tube.

To Use: *In northern latitudes, shadows point north at noon. Align the shadow of the upright pin to the N mark on the dial to determine direction.*

Native People

Historical Aid

The first Europeans to set foot on the land that would be Canada were met by many different tribes of Native People. The Micmac, Hurons, Algonquins, Iroquois, and Chippewa were just a few of the tribes that extended hospitality to the settlers and fur traders.

Early visitors depended on the natives for food, shelter, and medical help. The Native People of Canada lived close to and depended on nature. They taught settlers how to use the plants and trees for shelter, canoes, baskets, and mats. Many tribes farmed native crops like squash and beans. Early settlers were taught to tap the maple trees for "maple water" to make syrup and sugar.

> The Native People travelled the many waterways of Canada in canoes, some covered in hide and some made of birch bark. Overlapping sheets of birch bark were stretched over a framework of sapling strips, then sewn over the rim of the frame. Roots of the black spruce tree were used to sew everything into place. The bark was sewn together and curved pieces of cedar were lashed to the inside. Spruce gum was used to seal the seams from water. Planks of white cedar were used to line the inside. Wood ribs were fitted over the lining, and the outside of the canoe was water-sealed.

Project

Make a canoe like the ones used by Native People for transportation.

Materials

- Brown poster board or construction paper
- Canoe pattern, following
- Yarn   • Scissors
- Hole punch

Directions

1. Trace pattern onto poster board and cut out. Use hole punch to make holes where indicated on pattern.

2. Using yarn, lace ends of canoe together.

Canoe Pattern

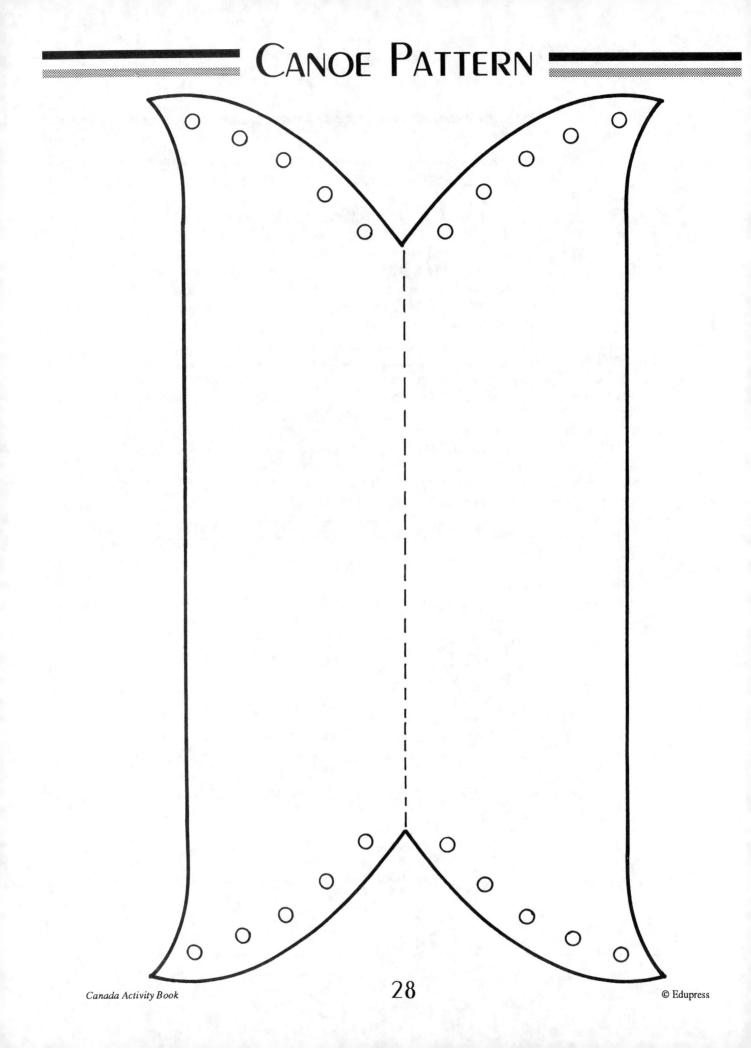

Native People

The Native People used whatever they had at hand for housing. The Micmac built grass lodgings called wigwams, which they would cover with furs in winter. Hides and birch bark were attached to wooden frames to make teepees.

Project

Make a wigwam like the ones used by Native People for shelter.

Directions

1. Turn container upside down. Cut small opening for door.

2. Tear construction paper into small pieces and glue in an overlapping pattern onto container.

3. Glue grass to paper-covered container, covering completely.

Materials

- Margarine or whipped cream container
- Glue
- Brown construction paper
- Dried grass, raffia, or straw

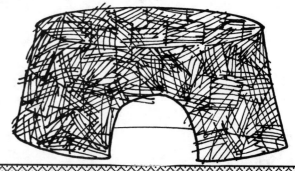

The Assiniboine depended on huge herds of bison for many of their needs. The Chippewa relied on caribou for the same needs. These huge animals supplied meat, hide for clothing and shelter, bone and sinew for tools and utensils. Meat was never wasted, but shared with the entire tribe. Horns were used for drinking cups, and hair from the neck was woven into rope, and combined with natural objects to make ornaments.

Project

Make a bison-hair bracelet.

Directions

1. Cut several lengths of yarn, 30 cm (12 in) long. Tie together at one end.

2. Braid the strands of yarn, threading shells into yarn at intervals.

3. Weave feathers into braid.

4. Tie ends of yarn together, adjusting to fit around wrist.

Materials

- Brown yarn or twine
- Small shells or other natural objects, drilled with a small hole
- Small feathers

FUR TRADING

Historical Aid

Felt hats were very popular in Europe beginning in the 17th century. The underfur of the Canadian beaver was perfect for making felt, and the demand for the animal grew. French and Scottish trappers led hunting expeditions into previously unexplored Canadian territory in search of these valuable animals. The fur traders fought bitter cold and disease. Meals consisted of cornmeal mush and pemmican flavored with hair, sticks, bark, and sand.

The Native People they befriended were given guns and traps in exchange for animal skins. They also traded for moccasins, buckskins, and canoes. Native inventions such as snowshoes and dog sleds enabled the fur traders to transport supplies and pelts when they might otherwise have failed.

Project

Play the role of a fur trader. Make a pair of snowshoes, then try to haul a heavy load of beaver pelts.

Materials

Snowshoes
- Heavy yarn or twine
- Poster board or cardboard
- Hole punch or nail

- Scissors
- Marking pen

Hauling sled
- Wagon
- Rope

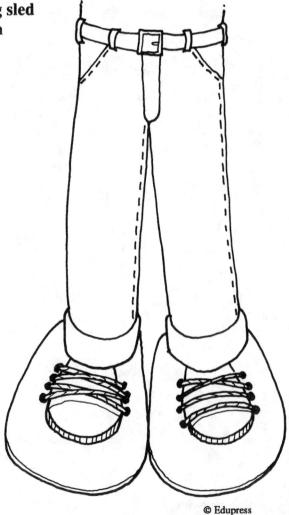

Directions

Snowshoes

1. Stand on the cardboard and have a partner trace around the outline of each foot.

2. Measure an oval 15.24 cm (6 in) larger than the outline and cut out the cardboard.

3. Make several holes on opposite sides of the arch area. Lace the holes with a long piece of yarn or twine. Step on the cardboard and tie it in place over your shoe.

Extended Activity

- *The natives' trained dogs could haul 272 kg (600 lb) loads a distance of 113 km (70 miles) a day. Pile a wagon with as many books or heavy objects as you can. Weigh each one before putting it in the wagon, then total the weight. Tie a rope to the wagon, put on your snowshoes, and pull your cargo. How much weight can you pull?*

Samuel de Champlain

Historical Aid

Samuel de Champlain was a Frenchman who first sailed to Canada in 1603. Five years later he returned to explore the St. Lawrence River. He chose a site on which to build a fort and trading post. It was named Quebec, the first permanent settlement in Canada.

The first winter was very cold, and even with the help of the Native People only eight of the 24 settlers survived. For ten years Champlain continued his explorations and his pursuit of a dream to build an empire. When he returned permanently to Quebec, he devoted himself to running the colony. With the help of Louis Hebert, known as Canada's first farmer, he created a garden where forest had been, and strengthened the growth of the settlement.

Project

Plant the same crops the first settlers of Quebec planted and harvested.

Materials

• Large plastic gardening containers
• Corn, pea, and bean seeds
• Planting soil
• Gardening tools
• Permanent marking pens

Directions

1. Fill the containers with soil.

2. Plant the seeds according to the directions on the package. Label each container.

3. Tend your small gardens. Water, fertilize, chart the growth.

Extended Activity

• *Imagine the difficulties the first settlers of Quebec faced when trying to grow crops in harsh winter weather. Experiment with a few of your "crops" by growing some in the classroom and some outdoors. Compare the results.*

SOIL

Hudson's Bay Company

Historical Aid

Two French fur traders founded the Hudson's Bay Company in 1670. They were given a royal charter and the exclusive right to trade with the Native People. At its largest, the Hudson's Bay Company controlled the area that stretched from Hudson Bay across Canada to the Pacific, and down into what became the state of Oregon. It extended north into the Arctic regions inhabited by the Inuits.

Hides, wild rice, and native handcrafted items were exchanged for European muskets, knives, wooden barrels, tools, and liquor. Native trappers were sometimes given a brass coin which had the value of one pelt. One side bore the likeness of King George IV. The other side pictured a beaver. A hole at the top enabled it to be worn as an ornament until redeemed at the company store.

Project

Reenact the trading between the Native People of Canada and the Europeans of the Hudson's Bay Company.

Materials

- Hudson's Bay Company project cards, following
- Materials as specified for each project
- Scissors
- Glue

Directions

1. Divide into two groups: Native People and Europeans. Divide each group into four smaller groups.

2. Cut the project cards apart. Give a card (1-4) to each Native People group. Give a card (5-8) to each European group.

3. Group members follow the directions for making the project described on their card.

4. Designate an area to be the trading post. Invite the Native People to visit the Europeans in the trading post and exchange goods.

HUDSON'S BAY COMPANY

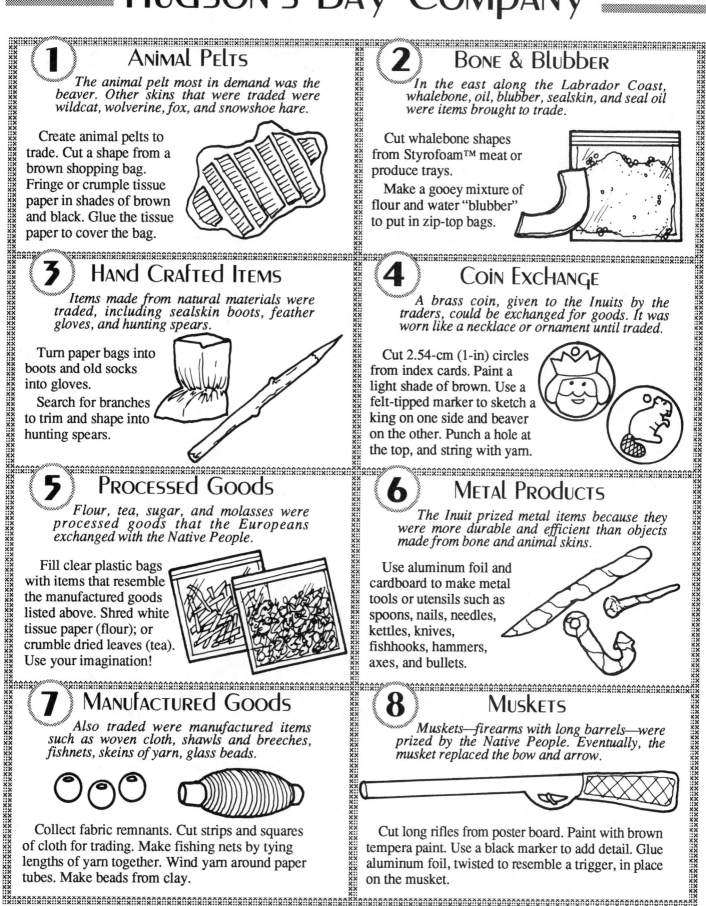

1 Animal Pelts

The animal pelt most in demand was the beaver. Other skins that were traded were wildcat, wolverine, fox, and snowshoe hare.

Create animal pelts to trade. Cut a shape from a brown shopping bag. Fringe or crumple tissue paper in shades of brown and black. Glue the tissue paper to cover the bag.

2 Bone & Blubber

In the east along the Labrador Coast, whalebone, oil, blubber, sealskin, and seal oil were items brought to trade.

Cut whalebone shapes from Styrofoam™ meat or produce trays.

Make a gooey mixture of flour and water "blubber" to put in zip-top bags.

3 Hand Crafted Items

Items made from natural materials were traded, including sealskin boots, feather gloves, and hunting spears.

Turn paper bags into boots and old socks into gloves.

Search for branches to trim and shape into hunting spears.

4 Coin Exchange

A brass coin, given to the Inuits by the traders, could be exchanged for goods. It was worn like a necklace or ornament until traded.

Cut 2.54-cm (1-in) circles from index cards. Paint a light shade of brown. Use a felt-tipped marker to sketch a king on one side and beaver on the other. Punch a hole at the top, and string with yarn.

5 Processed Goods

Flour, tea, sugar, and molasses were processed goods that the Europeans exchanged with the Native People.

Fill clear plastic bags with items that resemble the manufactured goods listed above. Shred white tissue paper (flour); or crumble dried leaves (tea). Use your imagination!

6 Metal Products

The Inuit prized metal items because they were more durable and efficient than objects made from bone and animal skins.

Use aluminum foil and cardboard to make metal tools or utensils such as spoons, nails, needles, kettles, knives, fishhooks, hammers, axes, and bullets.

7 Manufactured Goods

Also traded were manufactured items such as woven cloth, shawls and breeches, fishnets, skeins of yarn, glass beads.

Collect fabric remnants. Cut strips and squares of cloth for trading. Make fishing nets by tying lengths of yarn together. Wind yarn around paper tubes. Make beads from clay.

8 Muskets

Muskets—firearms with long barrels—were prized by the Native People. Eventually, the musket replaced the bow and arrow.

Cut long rifles from poster board. Paint with brown tempera paint. Use a black marker to add detail. Glue aluminum foil, twisted to resemble a trigger, in place on the musket.

The Gold Rush

Historical Aid

There were two major gold rushes in Canadian history. In 1858, prospectors found gold in the Cariboo Mountains in British Columbia. Miners made the difficult journey up the Fraser river to pan for gold along the shores of Quesnel and Cariboo Lakes, as well as along the many streams in the area.

In 1896, gold was discovered in the Klondike area of the Yukon. News of the Klondike gold strike was so exciting that prospectors came from all over North America to travel the "Road of 98." Prospectors reached the area either by travelling up the Yukon River through Alaska, or by trudging over the steep Coast Mountains through the White Pass or Chilkoot Pass. Miners had to walk in single file up steep "stairs" cut in the snow, carrying a year's worth of supplies on their back.

Panning was one of the most common ways to look for gold. A miner scooped a pan of dirt and gravel from a stream bed, stirred it to remove the lumps, then removed the rocks and pebbles. He would then wash away the most of the dirt by swirling the pan of water. He placed the remainder—gold dust, nuggets, and fine sand—in the sun or by a fire. When it was dry, he blew away the sand and had his gold.

Project

Practice panning for gold.

Materials

- Aluminum pie pan or iron skillet
- Aquarium gravel, spray-painted gold
- Mixture of sand and dirt
- Dish pans or large tub
- Water

Directions

1. Combine gravel, sand, dirt, and water in dish pans or tub.

2. Working on concrete outside, use the miners' method for panning for gold, spreading the remainders from the pan onto concrete to dry.

The Gold Rush

Prospectors who trudged over the Chilkoot and White Pass trails were not allowed to cross unless they carried with them enough supplies for an entire year. A mail-order catalog of the time sold a "Klondike Special" for $68.69 that included 227 kg (500 lbs) of flour, 90 kg (200 lbs) of bacon and .45 kg (one lb) of pepper. Many parts of the passes were too narrow and treacherous for pack animals—men would walk back and forth with their loads of supplies.

Project

Create a supply pack for a miner travelling over the Chilkoot Pass.

Materials

- Paper and pencil
- Food items, including flour and salt
- Empty grocery bags
- Pots, pans, cooking utensils
- Household items & tools (see directions)

Directions

1. As a class, brainstorm a list of things a prospector would need to live one year in the gold fields. Include food items, household items, and tools. Don't forget the equipment needed for prospecting!

2. Gather as many of the listed items as you can. (For food items such as flour, use empty grocery bags to represent the amount needed.)

3. Divide into groups, each group devising a plan to get the supplies over the mountain.

Extended Activity

- *Use measuring cups to measure various dry ingredients.*
- *How was food preserved for packing across the mountains? What kind of diet would a prospector most likely have?*

Northwest Passage

Historical Aid

Fur traders had searched many years for the fabled Northwest Passage, a waterway on which ocean-going ships could carry their furs across the northernmost parts of the Arctic, from the Atlantic to the Pacific.

Exploration was led by Captain James Cook, George Vancouver, and Alexander Mackenzie. Mackenzie became the first white man to travel overland from Canada's interior to the Pacific coast. Following maps and coastal charts filled with error and suggestion, the explorers finally realized that no such waterway existed. As a solution, the Canadian Pacific Railway, a transcontinental railroad, was built.

Project

Create a map showing a route through the northernmost Canadian territories.

Materials

• Poster board
• Colored pencils, marking pens, crayons

Directions

1. Imagine that you have heard stories about the Northwest Passage. Using the knowledge you have and stories you have heard about the Arctic, draw a map that charts the route you might take to find the Passage.

2. Start by making a list of the things you might encounter—ice, bays, islands, mountains, glaciers. Include them on the map.

NORTHWEST PASSAGE

The explorers searching for the Northwest Passage faced the harsh conditions of the Arctic. Some succeeded, others failed. The Royal Navy gave its exploring parties printed forms on which to record details of their journeys. Even though many did not survive, their stories could still be told through the journal entries.

PROJECT

Create a journal that retells the story of an Arctic expedition in search of the Northwest Passage.

MATERIALS

• Plain writing or drawing paper
• Colored pencils, marking pens, crayons
• Stapler

DIRECTIONS

1. Staple four sheets of writing paper together to form a booklet.

2. Share the stories of the three explorers told below. Retell the story in a picture journal.

Royal Navy Lieutenant Edward Parry—1819

Parry was the first Arctic explorer who deliberately spent a winter with his ships locked in the ice. The upper decks of his ships were roofed with quilted canvas. Heat was piped from the galley stoves. His crew existed on lime juice, vinegar, pickles, fresh bread, preserved fruits and soups, and beer brewed on ship. He sprouted seed for greens to prevent scurvy. The crew jogged on the enclosed decks and contributed articles and sketches to the expedition's newspaper.

Royal Navy Captain John Ross—1833

Ross and his crew survived in the Arctic longer than any Europeans before them. Three winters were spent with their ship trapped in the ice. They befriended the Inuit who taught them to adapt to the environment. They learned to build sleds and snow houses. They hunted seal and bear and used the hides to make clothing. They ate animal oil and fat.

Sir John Franklin—1847

Franklin began his expedition with 129 men, two ships and supplies for three years. When the ships became trapped in the ice, he sent a party ahead to search for a route they could take when the ice broke up. They used dogs to pull canoes over frozen lakes. Those staying behind set out in dories to navigate through large masses of ice. They ate pemmican and corn. Not one of the men who set out with Franklin was ever seen alive again.

FORESTRY

Historical Aid

Almost half of Canada's land is covered with forest. The forests are made up of many kinds of trees, including cedar, hemlock, fir, and pine. These trees provided most of the needs of the Native People: materials for homes and canoes; edible fruits and roots; leaves, bark, and mosses for medicines; shelter and food for the animals they hunted.

The lumber industry grew along with the fur trade as early settlers made their way across the Canadian frontier. Present-day Canada is still one of the leading lumber-producing nations of the world. The numerous lakes and rivers provide a natural transportation system for logs and other products of the industry. Christmas tree farms in Nova Scotia, Quebec, and New Brunswick send trees as far away as South America.

Project

Make a Canadian forest scene.

Materials

• White & brown construction paper
• Tissue paper in various shades of green
• Paint brush
• Scissors
• Liquid starch
• Glue

Directions

1. To make tree trunks, cut 2.54-cm (1 in) wide strips of brown construction paper. Glue in a vertical pattern to white construction paper.

2. Tear tissue paper into small pieces.

3. Brush each piece of tissue with liquid starch and place in an overlapping pattern to represent the leaves or needles on the trees.

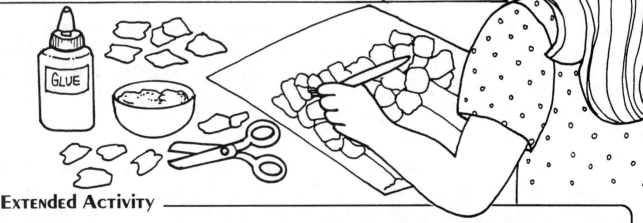

Extended Activity

• *Brainstorm a list of products that are part of the forestry industry—for example, paper and wood pulp. Look around the classroom and in your home for ideas.*

FORESTRY

The site of a log cabin sitting in a clearing is still very common, a reminder of life in Canada's past. Lumber from Canada's sawmills is shipped all over the country, as well as to faraway places like Japan.

Canadians proudly celebrate the heritage of their pioneer background. Festivals such as Klondike Days in Edmonton, Alberta, give Canadians an opportunity to test their skills as lumberjacks. Similar celebrations are held all across Canada. Contests might include sawing competitions and ox-pulls, in which oxen must pull heavy weights. In a log-rolling contest, two people balance on a log floating in water, each attempting to get the other dumped into the water!

PROJECT

Play a "lumberjack" relay game.

MATERIALS

- Plaid long-sleeved shirt and knit cap for each team
- Wooden boards, one per team
- Butcher paper
- Markers or crayons

DIRECTIONS

1. Divide into two or more teams.

2. Place the boards next to each other, several meters (yards) from the two teams. Place butcher paper either on an easel or a wall, on the opposite end of the boards from the teams' starting place.

3. The first runner on each team must put on the lumberjack's shirt and cap, then run to the board and walk across it. Be careful to keep your balance!

4. Once across, the runner goes to the butcher paper and draws a tree. (Good lumberjacks reforest the areas where they've been cutting!) He then recrosses the board, returns to his team, and passes the shirt and cap to the next person.

French Heritage

Historical Aid

Nearly one-quarter of the population of Canada is French-Canadian, most living in the province of Quebec. The provincial flag of Quebec features a *fleur-de-lis*, the traditional symbol of France. The French were the first to colonize the North Atlantic Coast, called New France, from the 14th century. It was the French who began the fur trade and were among the first pioneers to go into the Canadian wilderness.

French-Canadians of today, spread throughout Canada, still have deep ties with their past and their culture, which have always been closely tied to home, family, and church. Most speak French, and many choose to follow traditional occupations like fishing and farming. Traditional celebrations such as St. Jean Baptiste Day, and traditional foods, keep the French-Canadian culture united.

Project

Make an iris, or *fleur-de-lis*.

Directions

1. Trace pattern onto blue construction paper and cut out.

2. Alternating directions (up and down) curl individual petals around a pencil. Curl up-turning petals very tightly, down-turning petals more loosely.

3. Glue a few shreds of crepe paper into center of flower.

4. Roll green construction paper lengthwise into a tight tube and tape closed.

5. Make several 2.54 cm (1 in) slits in one end of tube, cutting through all layers.

6. Carefully extend the slits in the outermost layer of the paper tube to varying lengths. Fold these layers back to form leaves.

7. Fold remaining layers outward. Glue flower to the top of tube.

Materials

- Flower pattern, following
- Pencil
- Blue construction paper
- Green construction paper
- Yellow crepe paper, cut in small shreds
- Scissors • Tape • Glue

Scottish Heritage

Historical Aid

The population of Canada reflects many different cultures. In many cases, Canadians have held on to many aspects of their ancestors' heritage—customs, foods, and music. Nearly forty percent of modern Canadians are descended from settlers from the English and Scots who began to populate Canadian territories in the 1600s.

Across Canada, Scottish heritage is celebrated in *ceilidhs* and Highland Games. At these events, Canadians participate in Scottish dancing and athletics. One of the most popular events is tossing a heavy wooden pole called a *caber*. Participants often dress in kilts, a skirt-like garment made of special plaid fabrics called tartans.

Project

Design a tartan plaid and make a Scottish kilt.

Materials

- Butcher paper
- Yarn
- Stapler
- Colored markers
- Scissors

Directions

1. Measure butcher paper to fit around waist. Cut to fit. Measure yarn to fit around waist with enough extra to tie.

2. Choose three markers (two hot colors—red, yellow, or orange, and one cool color—blue, purple, or green).

3. Using all three colors, make a horizontal pattern of stripes, repeating pattern to cover paper.

4. Using two of the three colors, make a vertical pattern of stripes, repeating the pattern across the horizontal stripes.

5. Lay yarn along long edge of butcher paper. Fold paper over yarn and staple in place. Wrap around waist and tie to secure.

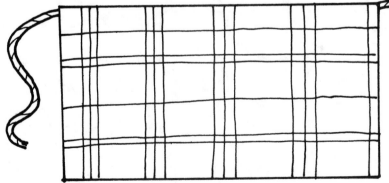

42

Winter Festivals

Historical Aid

Long, harsh winters are a part of Canadian life. Newcomers to this cold land learned to brighten the cold months with winter sports and recreation. By the nineteenth century, Canadians, especially those in Quebec, spent the winter in a frenzy of skating, sleighing, snowshoeing, snowball battles, and outdoor dances, concerts, and picnics.

North America's first winter carnival was staged in Montreal in 1833. Hundreds of people participated in five days of curling, sleigh-rides, tobogganing, snowshoeing, hockey, and fireworks. Later festivals featured elaborate ice palaces, carved from huge pieces of ice.

Project

Celebrate winter with snowball fun. If no snow is available, use wadded paper or foam balls.

Snowball Battle
Divide into two teams. Establish basic rules for safety and fun, and start throwing!

Snowball Tower
Stack snowballs, competing to see who can make the highest stack.

Snowball Race
Divide into teams and challenge each other to see which team can make the most snowballs (from snow or paper) in five minutes!

Calgary Stampede

Historical Aid

For one week during every summer the citizens of Calgary, Alberta, don western clothes and cowboy hats to celebrate the history of the old frontier with the Calgary Stampede. Calgary was built on the frontier economy of cattle, wheat, oil, and natural gas. This yearly rodeo event celebrates the city's history.

The entire city is redecorated to look like an old western town, and it is not unusual to find horses in the streets and tethered to parking meters. The streets are filled with music coming from loudspeakers. People come from all over the world to watch bucking broncos, steer-wrestling, wild-horse races, and chuck wagon races.

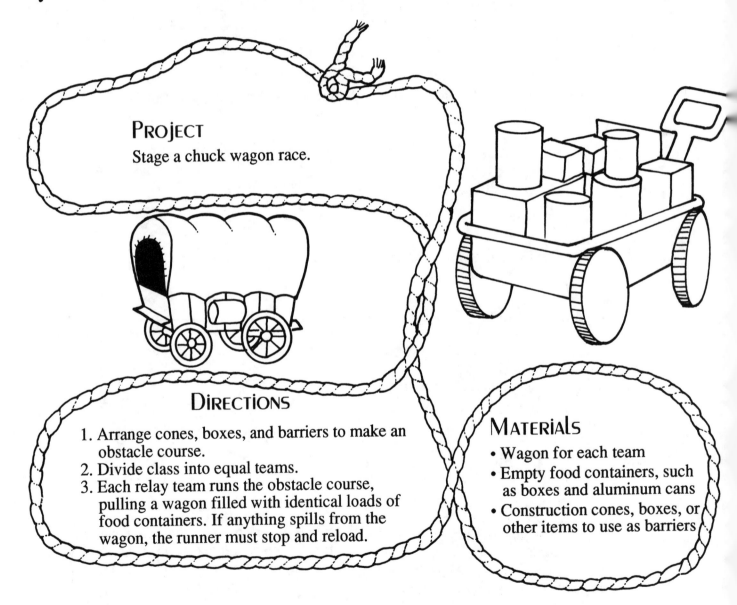

Project
Stage a chuck wagon race.

Directions
1. Arrange cones, boxes, and barriers to make an obstacle course.
2. Divide class into equal teams.
3. Each relay team runs the obstacle course, pulling a wagon filled with identical loads of food containers. If anything spills from the wagon, the runner must stop and reload.

Materials
- Wagon for each team
- Empty food containers, such as boxes and aluminum cans
- Construction cones, boxes, or other items to use as barriers

Canada Activity Book   © Edupress

INUIT

Historical Aid

The Inuit are the Native People of Canada's far north. Known by their ancient enemies as *Eskimos* (eaters of raw meat), Inuit (the people) was their own name for themselves. Blubber, meat, and fish were often eaten raw by these people, because material for fire-building was so scarce.

The extreme Arctic weather conditions in which the Inuits lived forced them to be inventive with natural resources in order to survive. Caribou antlers and hides provided the materials for harpoons, sleds, and clothing. Seal oil was used for fuel. Houses, called *igloos*, were built from compact snow cut with an ivory knife into blocks and stacked to form a dome. Driftwood was the only wood available. Fire was made by striking chunks of pyrite together and catching the sparks in grass. Soapstone was patiently carved into cooking pots.

Project

Build an Inuit igloo.

Materials

- Self-hardening clay
- White paint suitable for painting clay
- Waxed paper
- Paint brush
- Plastic knives

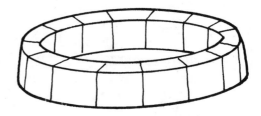

Directions

1. Form the clay into 1.25-cm (½-inch) blocks.

2. Use the plastic knife to trim the sides into flat edges.

3. On the waxed paper, form a circle with the clay blocks. Cut them to slope as shown in the illustration. Continue stacking the clay blocks, sloping inward with each row. Smooth and trim the sides. When the dome shape is finished and the clay has hardened, paint the igloo white.

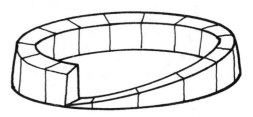

Igloo Facts

- *The entrance to the igloo was usually a tunnel.*
- *Outside cracks were wedged with snow.*
- *Inside walls were rubbed with snow, then glazed with flame.*
- *A winter igloo usually measured 4.6 meters (15 ft) across and 3.7 meters (12 ft) high.*

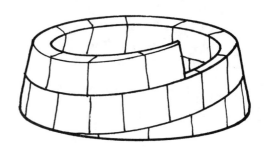

Pacific Northwest Tribes

Historical Aid

The native tribes of the Pacific Northwest lived in great wooden lodges built amidst forests of firs, cedars, and redwoods. They caught salmon, whales, and halibut for food and wore clothes of sea otter and fur. Among these tribes were the Haida, Tsimshian, Kwakiutl, Bella Coola, and Nootka. They developed great artistic skills, expressing themselves through woodworking. Examples of their fine work appeared in totem poles, jewelry, and elaborate masks.

It is believed that George Vancouver, a Royal Navy officer mapping the Pacific Coastline in 1788, was the first European explorer to meet these friendly coastal inhabitants.

Project

Choose one or more crafts to complete.

Animal Deities

Animal deities were featured in many tribal crafts, dances, and ceremonies. Images were carved into the trunks of massive trees to create totem poles or statues to guard the grave of a chief. Dressed in a feather costume and beaked mask, a dancer would assume the role of a mythological bird and perform a wing-flapping ritual at the start of wedding festivities or coming-of-age ceremonies.

Project

1. Use construction paper, cardboard, glue, paper plates, grocery bags, and other craft materials to create a colorful ceremonial mask to represent an imaginative animal or bird.

2. Attach yarn, if necessary, on the sides of the mask to tie it around the head.

Canada Activity Book

© Edupress

Potlatch

Important tribal events provided the occasion for a potlatch—a ceremony at which a chief demonstrated his wealth by lavishing expensive gifts on his rivals. Each recipient hosted his own potlatch at which he sought to provide gifts of greater value. A chief might distribute as many as 30,000 blankets or 10,000 silver and brass bracelets or jade ornaments. These potlatches became so competitive and wasteful that the Canadian government outlawed them in 1884.

PROJECT

Create a jeweled ornament.

1. Cut an unusual shape from butcher paper.

2. Decorate the shape with bright paint, sequins, and other trims.

3. Give the ornament away during a classroom potlatch.

Cedar

Cedar was the basis of the native culture. Huge trunks provided the material for dugout canoes up to 23 meters (75 feet) long and holding 50 paddlers. They framed houses 18 meters (60 feet) wide and 91 meters (300 feet) long. Shredded bark was woven into cloaks to wear in the rain. Bright geometric designs were carved into masks, totem poles, and cedar chests in which chiefs stored their blankets.

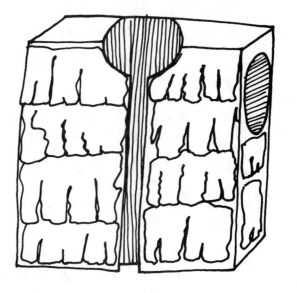

PROJECT

Design a cedar bark cloak.

1. Cut the center of a large brown shopping bag from bottom to top. Cut neck and arm holes.

2. Shred another shopping bag or brown tissue paper. Glue to the bag to create a shaggy appearance.

Glossary

Acadians—French settlers in the area now known as Nova Scotia.

ceilidh—a celebration featuring Scottish music and dance.

deity—a god.

fleur-de-lis—the ancient French symbol that appears on the flag of Quebec. The name means "flower of the lily," and its shape resembles an iris.

habitant—the rural farmers of New France.

House of Commons—one of the two bodies of Parliament. Members are elected by the Canadian people.

lumberjack—a person whose work is to cut down timber and prepare it for the sawmill.

Micmac—Native People of eastern Canada. First encountered by Cartier in his explorations, they helped the European settlers adapt to life in New France.

New France—the name given to Canada by the first European explorers.

Northwest Passage—the legendary water route across the North American continent that many explorers hoped to find.

pemmican—food substance made of dried meat and berries, kneaded together with fat and shaped into patties. It could be stored for long periods of time and was easy to take on long expeditions.

potlatch—celebration at which a chief of the Native People displays his wealth with food and gifts.

Quebecois—the French-speaking residents of Quebec.

Senate—one of the two bodies of Parliament. Members are appointed by the Governor-General.

tartan—a plaid pattern with stripes of different widths and colors originally worn by the Scots in Scotland. Each clan, or group of families, has its own pattern.

totem—animal or natural object taken as a symbol for a family or clan.

voyageur—French term for the adventurers who explored unknown areas of Canada in search of animal pelts for trading.

wigwam—a type of tent used by some tribes of Native People. It is shaped in a dome or cone and covered with bark, grass, woven mats, leaves, or other natural material.